GOLF *FORE!!* KIDS

by STEPHEN J. RUTHENBERG

Illustrations by
Joel Beals

RGS PUBLISHING
Lansing, Michigan

Additional copies of this book may be orderd through
bookstores or by calling:
ACCESS PUBLISHING
6893 Sullivan Road
Grawn, Michigan 49637
1-800-507-BOOK
(Phone Line Open 24 Hours)
or
1-800-345-0096

Front cover photograph by Gary Shrewsbury
Illustrations by Joel Beals

Copyright 1997 by Stephen J. Ruthenberg

All rights reserved. No part of this book may be reproduced by
any means, without permission in writing from the publisher,
except by a reviewer who wishes to quote brief excerpts. For
information contact RGS Publishing, P.O. Box 25021, Lansing,
Michigan, 48909.

Publisher's Cataloging-in-Publication Data

Ruthenberg, Stephen J. , 1961-
    Golf "fore" kids / by
    Stephen J. Ruthenberg.-- Lansing, Michigan:
    RGS Publishing.
        p.   ill.   cm.
    ISBN 0-9631514-3-6
    1. Golf.   I. Title.   II. Title: Golf fore kids.
    III. Title: Golf for kids.

    1997   96-067461
First Printing 1997

10 9 8 7 6 5 4 3

Manufactured in the United States of America

For three great kids;
Jason, Amy and Kaitlin,
For a wonderful wife;
Karen,
For my father;
Michael Ruthenberg
who never lost the kid in him.

ACKNOWLEDGMENTS

This book was made possible with the help of many people. A special thanks to Joel Beals for developing the many fine illustrations, which are the heart of this book. Also, thanks to Matt Stehouwer, Brooks Lance, Kim Miller and the Thompson Shore Staff for their patience in getting me through the electronic pre-press. Thanks to Cheryl Rasmussen for her excellent assistance in the layout and editing of the book along with Gary Shrewsbury for producing another great cover photo.

Thanks to my wife Karen for her helpful input. Also, thanks to the many editors for making this a better book. Last, thanks to the kids that helped with the photographing to prepare the illustrations. Thanks to Jason Jecks, Amy Ruthenberg, Greg and Megan Balsdon, Deven O'Connor, Shelby Colston, Chris Krol, Megan and Lauren Wesley, Mike Kahl, Grant Tungate and Brett Holmes.

CONTENTS

ABOUT THE AUTHOR

Stephen Ruthenberg has over 20 years of experience in the golf business. He has been a member of the Professional Golfers Association of America for 10 years. Currently, Steve is the Head Golf Professional at Michigan State University's Forest Akers Golf Courses.

In 1992, Steve authored the book "Golf Fore Beginners" which is published in both the English and Japanese language. Steve enjoys teaching the game of golf to people of all ages and abilities at The Golf Center at Michigan State University.

ABOUT THE ILLUSTRATOR

Joel Beals is from Grand Blanc, Michigan. He received his B.A. in Studio Art from Michigan State University and his M.F.A. in Medical and Biological Illustration from the University of Michigan. He is currently employed as a medical illustrator.

INTRODUCTION

Welcome !!! As a golf instructor, I am excited to introduce to you the great game of golf.   My golf ball friend and I have a lot of fun information we would like to share with you. I will provide most of the instruction, and our friend will give you some interesting *Tips* and *Fun Facts* about the game.

With the introduction of our golf ball friend you are invited to participate in the contest to give him a name. See page 124 for details.

Playing golf can be lots of fun!! So let's go to the golf course and learn more about the game.

Your Golf Instructor

Coach Ruthenberg

CHAPTER 1
THE WONDERFUL WORLD OF GOLF

 Welcome to the wonderful world of golf!!! Golf is often called a lifetime game, because you can play it regardless of your age. This sport is enjoyed by millions of boys and girls, and men and women throughout the world. You can play with your friends, parents, grandparents, brothers and sisters. You can even play the game by yourself.

Golf is played on a large, beautiful piece of land called a *golf course*. Golf courses provide homes for various wildlife like birds, ducks, squirrels and frogs. Many different types of plants, trees and flowers also grow on the golf course.

When arriving at a golf course you should always check-in and pay at the *golf shop* first.

THE OBJECT OF THE GAME

The object of the game of golf is to hit a *golf ball* into a *hole*. You hit the golf ball with different *golf clubs* called *woods*, *irons*, and *putters*. Each attempt to hit the golf ball is called a *stroke*. The fewer strokes it takes to get the ball into the hole, the better your score.

CHAPTER 2
THE PLAYING FIELD

Many sports are played on a standardized play-ing surface. For example, a football field, basket-ball court, and tennis court are always the same. Golf is different. Every golf course is different, because the lay of the land, trees and vegitation, and the layout of every hole is unique.

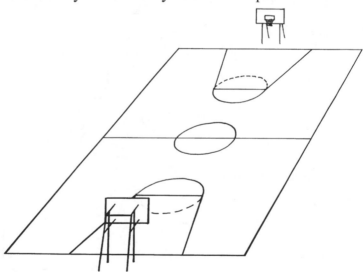

Every golf course consists of 9 or 18 different holes. Each hole varies in *design, length,* and *character.* As shown below, the starting point for each hole is the *tee,* which is located on the *teeing ground.* The finishing point for each hole is the *hole,* also called the *cup,* which is found on the *green.*

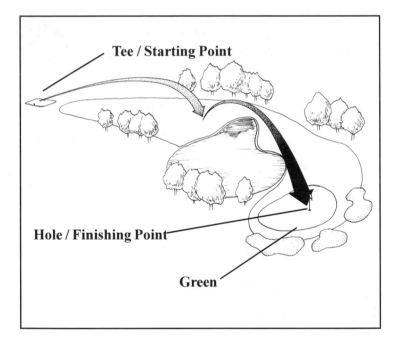

THE TEEING GROUND

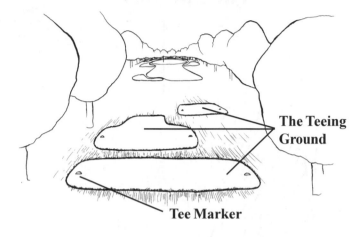

The Teeing Ground

Tee Marker

The *tee markers* located on the teeing ground are the starting points of the hole. Normally each hole has between three to five sets of tee markers, with each set being a different color. Each set of tee markers are located on a different part of the teeing ground. The hole can be easier or harder depending on which set of markers you play from. Your *scorecard* and the *tee-sign* located on the teeing ground usually show the length of each hole from each set of tee markers.

TIP: As a junior golfer, begin playing each hole from the set of tees closest to the green, or even closer. As your skills improve, you may play from farther back.

The Fairway

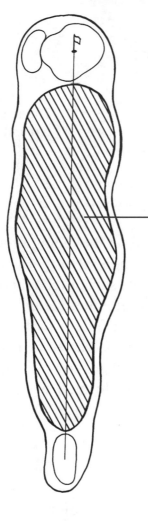

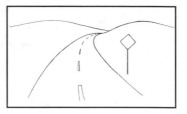

The Fairway

The *fairway* is the easiest route to follow, to get from the tee to the green. It is like the "road" to the green.

The grass in the fairway is usually cut shorter than the grass surrounding the fairway. Therefore, it is normally easier to hit the ball from the fairway, than from the area surrounding the fairway.

The Rough

The *rough* is the area of the course that borders and surrounds the fairway. If you hit your golf ball into the rough, you may get into *long grass, trees, mounds* or *hazards*. It will usually be more difficult to hit your ball out of these areas. If possible, avoid this area and try to keep your ball in the fairway.

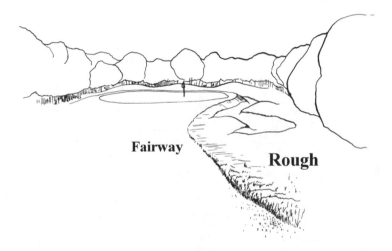

Fairway

Rough

Hazards

Hazards, as defined in the "Rules for Golf", are either *water hazards* or *bunkers*.

WATER HAZARDS

A water hazard is a body of water that could be as large as the ocean or as small as a creek. You can find water hazards on the course in the form of lakes, oceans, ponds, rivers and creeks.

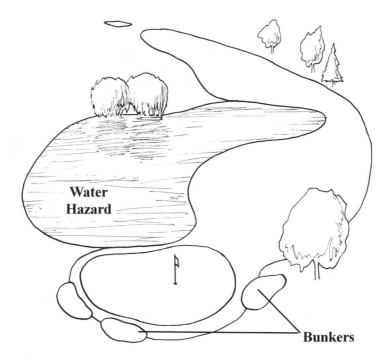

BUNKERS

A bunker is a hole in the land, often filled with sand. You may have heard them called "Sand Traps", but the proper name is a *bunker*. Bunkers often border the fairway and surround the green. Bunkers next to the fairway are called *fairway bunkers* and those next to the green are called *greenside bunkers*. They come in many different shapes and sizes. You will find it is difficult to hit good golf shots out of bunkers.

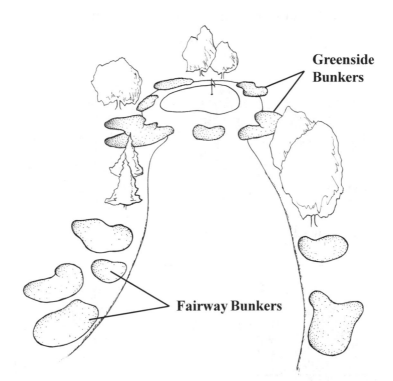

Greenside Bunkers

Fairway Bunkers

The Green

Located on the green is the *hole,* or *cup*. As mentioned before, the object of the game is to get your golf ball into the hole, or cup. The hole is identified by a *flagstick*.

The grass on the green is different than the grass that grows in the yards of most homes. The name of the two most common types of grass used on greens is called *bentgrass* or *bermuda grass*. To make the ball roll easier, the grass is normally cut shorter on the green then any other part of the course.

The border around the green is referred to as the *fringe*, *apron*, or *collar*.

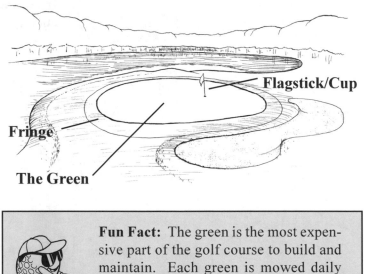

Flagstick/Cup

Fringe

The Green

Fun Fact: The green is the most expensive part of the golf course to build and maintain. Each green is mowed daily with a special type of mower.

Out of Bounds

Being *out of bounds* is when your golf ball lands in the area surrounding the golf course that you are not allowed to play from. The "out of bounds" is marked with white stakes, posts, or fences.

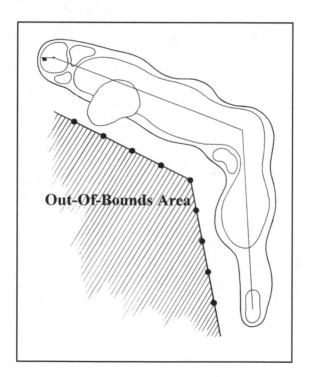

A Golf Hole

See if you can name the parts of the golf hole below.

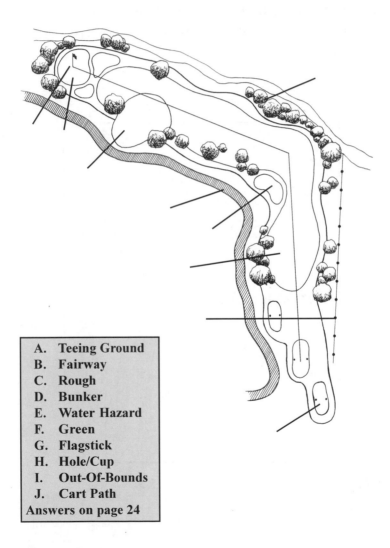

A. **Teeing Ground**
B. **Fairway**
C. **Rough**
D. **Bunker**
E. **Water Hazard**
F. **Green**
G. **Flagstick**
H. **Hole/Cup**
I. **Out-Of-Bounds**
J. **Cart Path**
Answers on page 24

Par

All holes are assigned a *par* which is a score of excellence when playing the hole. Par is always *three*, *four* or *five,* depending on the *length* of the hole. The chart below shows the guidelines for determining the par of a hole. As a beginner, you will find it very difficult to score par or even close to par on any hole.

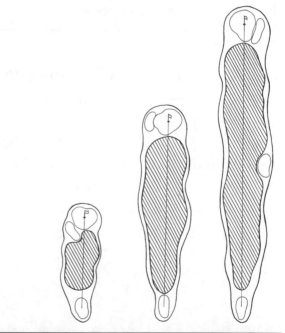

Par	3	4	5
Men's Yardage	Up to 250 yds	251-470 yds	Over 471 yds
Women's Yardage	Up to 210 yds	211-400 yds	401-575 yds

Fun Fact : A par three is designed so you can get on the green in one shot, then have two putts to get the ball into the hole. A par four is designed to get on the green in two shots, and a par five is designed to get on the green in three shots. As a junior golfer, it is rare to reach the green in this number of shots. However, as you grow stronger, you will be able to get to the green in the correct number of shots.

Golf's Unit of Measurement

The *yard* is the unit of measurement used in golf. **One yard = 3 feet or 36 inches.** A golf hole is measured in yards, starting from the tee markers to the middle of the green. Also, how far you hit the ball is measured in yards.

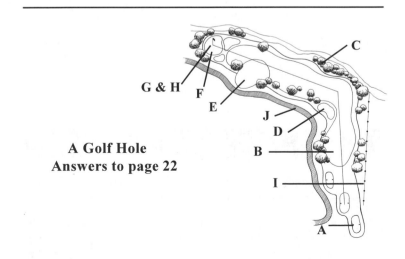

A Golf Hole
Answers to page 22

TERM TIME

APRON: Grass bordering the green, normally slightly higher than the grass on the green. Also called fringe or collar.

BLIND SHOT: When the spot that you want to hit the ball to is not visible when taking your shot.

BUNKER: A hazard near the green or fairway with a depression or mounding in the landscape, which is often filled with sand.

DOGLEG: A golf hole that curves to the left or right.

FLAGSTICK OR FLAG: A tall pole with a flag at the top to mark the location of the hole on the green.

GREEN: The closely-mowed surface where the hole, or cup, is located. The putter is the only type of club you should use on the green.

HAZARD: Any bunker or body of water marked on the course. Most, but not all, hazards are in the rough.

OUT-OF-BOUNDS: The area marked with white stakes, posts, or a fence where play is prohibited.

ROUGH: The long grass and other vegetation surrounding the fairway and the green.

CHAPTER 3
TOOLS FOR GOLF

To play the game of golf you need the right tools or *equipment*. This chapter will introduce you to the equipment used for playing golf.

The Golf Ball

First, you need a *golf ball*. The golf ball is usually white or other bright colors so it is easy to find in the grass. The small circles or patterns covering the outside of the ball are called *dimples*. Dimples help the ball fly.

FUN FACT: Did you know the dimples on different golf balls come in different shapes, sizes and patterns. Today the average golf ball has over 350 dimples.

What You Swing

Next, you need *clubs* to hit the golf ball around the golf course. There are three different types of golf clubs: *woods, irons,* and *putters*. You will use different clubs to hit the golf ball depending on how far you want the ball to go and where you are located on the golf course.

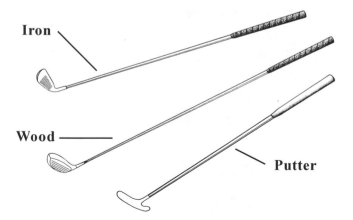

Iron

Wood

Putter

PUTTERS

When playing golf you will need a *putter*. The putter is used to hit the golf ball when the ball is on or within a few feet the of putting green. Putters come in different shapes and sizes as shown below.

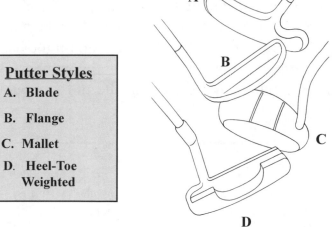

Putter Styles

A. **Blade**

B. **Flange**

C. **Mallet**

D. **Heel-Toe Weighted**

IRONS

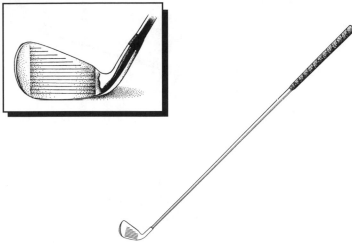

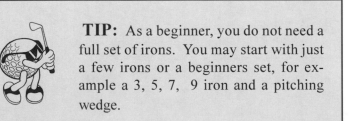

Irons are designed to hit the ball farther than your putter. When playing golf you need different irons to hit the ball different distances. Irons are identified with different numbers from 1-9, a pitching wedge and a sand wedge. The lower the number of the iron, the farther the club can hit the ball. Irons normally come in a set, with the numbers 3-9 and a pitching wedge, being the most popular set.

TIP: As a beginner, you do not need a full set of irons. You may start with just a few irons or a beginners set, for example a 3, 5, 7, 9 iron and a pitching wedge.

The illustration below shows how the flight of a golf ball will vary with different clubs. For example, when using a 3-iron the ball will go farther, but not as high as a 5-iron. As you can see with the clubs shown below, you would use a 7-iron or a 9-iron as you get closer to the green.

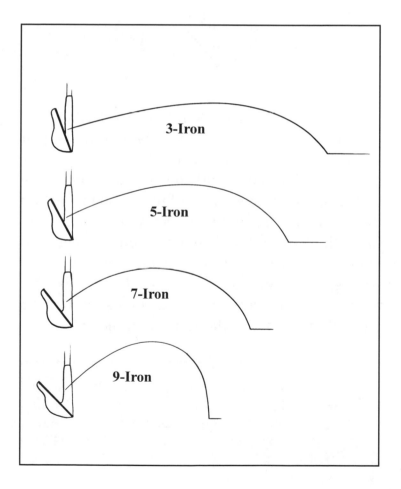

WOODS

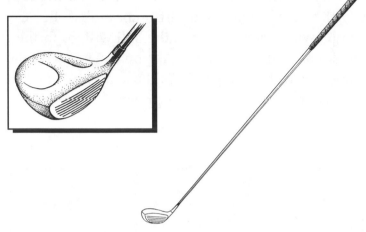

Woods are designed to hit the ball farther than both a putter and most irons. Just like irons, you use different woods to hit the ball different distances. Each wood is marked with a different number. The lower the number of the wood the farther the ball should go. For example, a 3-wood is made to hit the ball farther than a 5-wood. Along with your irons, a set of clubs normally includes three woods, a 1, 3 and 5-wood. The 1-wood is normally called a *driver*, because you use it to drive the ball off the tee at the start of a hole.

FUN FACT: Woods are called woods because for many years the clubhead of all woods were made from actual wood. Today, most woods are made from metals.

As with irons, the illustration below shows how clubheads get smaller and; the clubface angle increases with each wood as the number gets higher. It also shows how the flight of the ball changes with each wood.

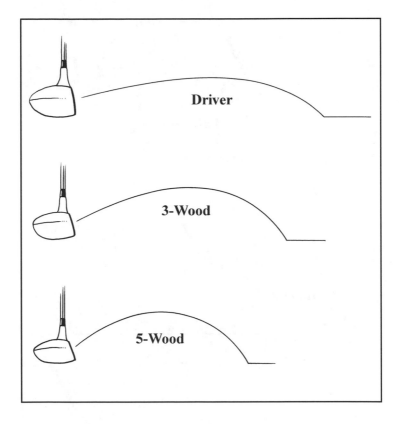

PARTS OF A GOLF CLUB

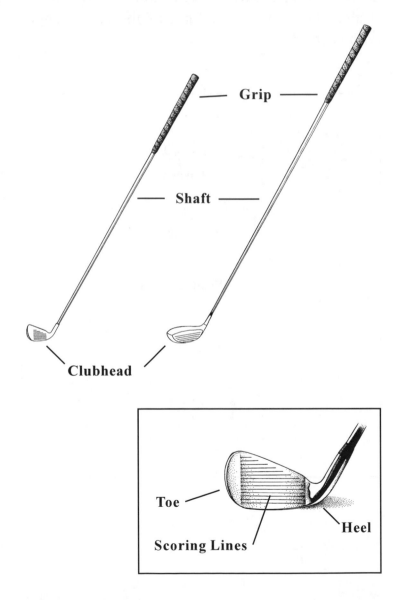

Grip

Shaft

Clubhead

Toe

Scoring Lines

Heel

A SET OF CLUBS

The illustration below shows an example of a complete set of golf clubs. As a beginner, you may start with as few as four clubs which include; one wood (a three or five wood), two irons (a five and nine) and a putter. As you get older and improve your skills you can add clubs to your starter set.

| 1 | 3 | 5 | 3 | 4 | 5 | 6 | 7 | 8 | 9 | PW | SW |

WOODS **IRONS** **WEDGES**

FUN FACT: The <u>Rules Of Golf</u> allow you to play with up to, but no more than, 14 clubs in your golf bag.

CLUB FITTING

When batting in baseball all children do not use a bat that is the same size or weight. This same principle applies in golf. It is very important to make sure your golf clubs fit you correctly. First, to properly fit, your clubs should have the correct grip size so you can hold the club correctly. Next, the length and weight of the club must also match your height and strength. Also, the angle the shaft comes out from the clubhead to your hands must fit you correctly. Last, the flexibility of the shaft should match your swing speed.

When buying clubs check with your local golf professional or clubfitter to make sure the clubs you are buying fit you correctly. As you grow taller and stronger your clubs will also need to be changed accordingly.

PARENT TIP: Today there are many different junior sets of clubs available at golf stores for children of various ages. You can also have used clubs cut down and put junior grips on them. If you choose the latter, make sure the weight of the club you cut down is not to heavy.

OTHER GOLF EQUIPMENT

The illustration below shows other equipment you may use when playing golf.

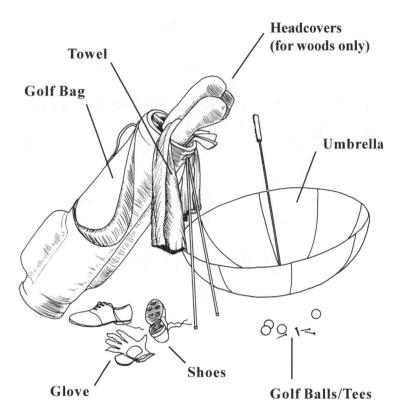

<u>TERM TIME</u>

CLUBFACE: The part of the club that makes contact with the ball.

DRIVER: Another term for the 1-wood.

FLANGE: The bottom or sole of the club.

GRIP: The part of the club that you hold in your hands.

HEEL: The area of the clubhead near the neck or shaft of the club.

LOFT OF THE CLUB: The angle of the clubface. This angle effects the height and distance of your golf shot.

NECK: The area where the shaft meets the clubhead.

CHAPTER 4
THE RULES OF GOLF

Like all other sports or games, there are rules to follow when playing the game of golf. Most sports have a person or persons to officiate the game so all participants follow the rules. For example, baseball has umpires. Football, basketball, and hockey have referees. Golf is different because you and the people you play with are your own officials.

When playing in a golf tournament if you break the rules or see one of your opponents break the rules, you must inform your playing opponent and a rules official of the infraction. Therefore, honesty and trust are important when playing golf. Since you are your own official in golf, you should learn the rules of the game.

The rules of golf are in a book called *The Rules Of Golf.*

There are many rules to cover many situations that can happen when playing golf. We are going to learn just a few of the rules of golf so you can start playing the game correctly.

The rules in the book are determined by two important golf organizations. These organizations are the *United States Golf Association* and the *Royal and Ancient Golf Association of St. Andrews, Scotland.* Every two years these two organizations meet to determine if there needs to be any changes to the rules of golf.

RULE 1

On each teeing ground there are *tee markers*. When starting each hole you should put the ball between the tee markers and not in front of the markers. The illustration below shows how the ball can be put between the markers and up to *two-club lengths behind* the tee markers.

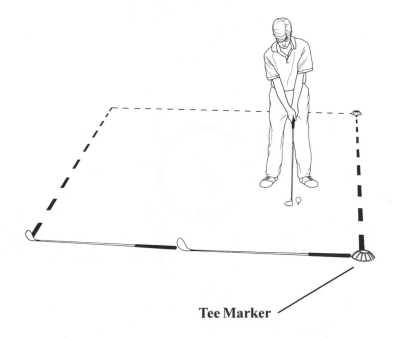

Tee Marker

RULE 2

Except for some special situations, you are *not* allowed to touch the ball, or improve the position of the ball, from the time you hit from the tee, until you get the ball in the hole on the green.

 **RULES TIP:** When you are on the green you may mark your golf ball with a coin or a marker and lift your golf ball to clean it. You cannot do this on any other part of the golf course other than the green.

RULE 3

When putting on the green, the flagstick must be *out* of the hole when the ball goes into the hole. If your ball hits the flagstick when you are putting on the green, you get a two stroke penalty. This means you must add two strokes to your score for that hole.

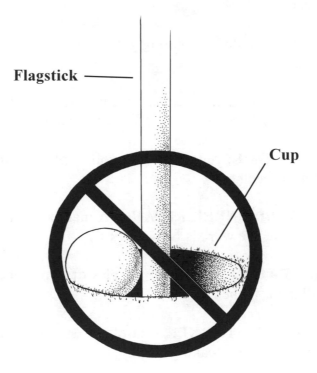

Flagstick ———

Cup

<u>Term Time</u>

ADDRESSING THE BALL: The position a player takes in preparing to hit the ball.

CADDIE: A person that carries a players golf equipment and helps with the club selection and strategy of play.

CASUAL WATER: A puddle of water, not in a water hazard.

CUP: The hole on a putting green; 4 and 1/4 inches in diameter.

FORECADDIE: A person assigned to help spot where the golf balls land for players in a tournament.

FOURSOME: A group of four golfers playing a round of golf together.

GROUND UNDER REPAIR: A marked area of the course where work is being done.

HOLE-OUT: To complete the play of a hole when the ball lands in the cup.

PENALTY STROKE: A stroke or strokes added to your score for breaking a rule.

CHAPTER 5
MINDING YOUR
MANNERS -
GOLF ETIQUETTE

Have you ever heard of the word *etiquette*? This is something golfers have been practicing for hundreds of years. ***Etiquette means polite behavior.*** As a golfer, it is important to be polite on the golf course at all times. You should practice etiquette to anyone on the course and to the golf course itself.

SAFETY TIPS

Golf can be dangerous if not played correctly. The following safety tips will help keep you safe when on the course.

THE WORD "FORE"

Fore is what you should yell if you hit a golf ball and it accidently goes towards another golfer. Make sure to yell as loud as you can so that they will hear you. If you are on the course and you hear someone yell fore, you should put your head down and turn away from the sound as in the picture below. When on the course, always be aware of golfers around you.

WHERE TO STAND

When another player is hitting you should stand back and to the side of where the person is hitting, as shown below.

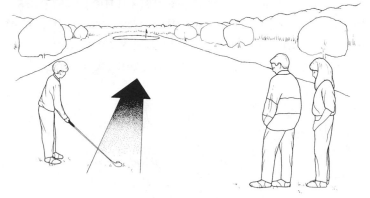

The next illustration shows where you should **<u>not</u>** stand.

LIGHTNING

If you are on a golf course and you see lightning, you should immediately walk or run to the clubhouse or seek proper shelter on the golf course. Some courses provide weather shelters at different locations on the course. Do not stay under a tree for protection because trees attract lightning.

Never go under a tree if there is lightning on the course

MAINTAINING THE COURSE

By taking care of the golf course, you and other golfers will enjoy the game even more. The following suggestions will help you better maintain the golf course.

REPLACE YOUR DIVOTS

Sometimes when hitting a golf ball you will remove a piece of grass from the ground. The grass that you remove from the ground is called a *divot*. By replacing your divots, the grass will grow back quicker. When golfers replace their divots, there is less chance for a golf ball to land in a bare spot on the golf course.

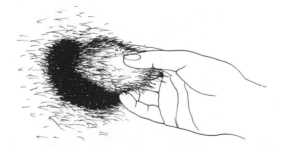

 **TIP:** To help reduce divots on the teeing area, never take practice swings on the tee. If you are waiting to tee off and would like to take some practice swings, step to the side of the teeing ground.

RAKING BUNKERS

After hitting your ball out of a bunker, rake your footprints as you are walking out of the bunker. This will provide a better lie for the next golfer that hits their ball into the bunker. Also, enter and exit the bunker as close to the ball as you can. This will reduce the amount of raking you will have to do.

 **TIP:** If your ball comes to rest in a foot print in the bunker, you must play the ball as it lies without moving it. This is why it is important to rake the bunker and remove your foot prints for the next golfer.

FIXING BALL MARKS

Sometimes when the ball lands on the green it will leave a dent called a *ball mark* on the green. To keep the green healthy, always fix your ball mark on the green. You can fix a ball mark with a ball mark repair tool or a tee, as shown below.

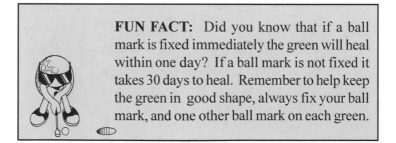

FUN FACT: Did you know that if a ball mark is fixed immediately the green will heal within one day? If a ball mark is not fixed it takes 30 days to heal. Remember to help keep the green in good shape, always fix your ball mark, and one other ball mark on each green.

GENERAL ETIQUETTE

ORDER OF PLAY

For each hole, the person that had the lowest score on the previous hole gets to hit first. This person is said to have the *honor*. If you tied on the last hole, then go to the score on the hole before to decide.

During the play of a hole, the person that is farthest away from the hole should always go first.

WHEN TO HIT

Before hitting, always make sure that there are no golfers close enough to get hit by your shot. Start the hole as soon as you can without hitting anyone.

TALKING & RUNNING

You should not talk when other golfers are swinging because this will disturb them. Also, do not run on the golf course.

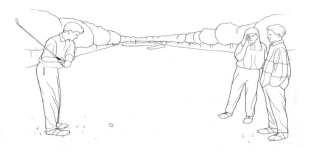

PLAYING THROUGH

Sometimes when playing golf, the group be-hind you plays faster than your group. It is polite to let that group *play through* and continue the round of golf in front of you. After your tee shot, step aside and let them tee and go ahead of you.

ON THE PUTTING GREEN

Marking your ball

Marking your ball is when you put a coin or ball mark on the green in the place of your ball. If your ball is in the way of another golfer's ball when they are putting, you should always mark your ball. You may clean your golf ball after you mark it on the green.

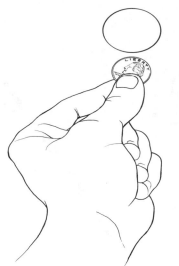

Tending the Flag

When putting, if you are too far from the hole to see it clearly, you may have another golfer or caddie *"tend the flag"*. "Tending the flag" is when someone holds the flag in the hole while you putt, so that you can see where the hole is. Then, when you putt the ball, the flag is pulled out of the hole before the ball gets to the hole. Remember, if your ball hits the flagstick, even when having someone "tend the flag", you need to add two strokes to your score!

Walking Around The Hole

When walking near the hole do not step on the hole. Walk around the hole.

The Flagstick

When putting on the green the golf ball cannot hit the flagstick whether the flagstick is in the hole or lying on the green. Therefore, when the flagstick is removed from the hole make sure it is not left near the hole or anywhere that will interfere with another golfer's putt as shown below.

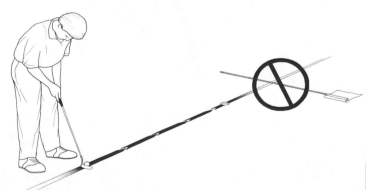

A good place to put the flagstick when it is removed, is on the fringe around the green.

The Line Of A Putt

Every putt has an imaginary line or path that it will follow to the hole. Do not walk or step on this imaginary line, whether it is the line of your putt or another golfer's.

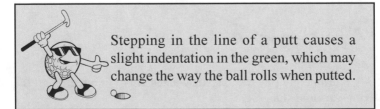

Stepping in the line of a putt causes a slight indentation in the green, which may change the way the ball rolls when putted.

When another player is getting set-up to putt, do not stand along the line or path of the ball, because this may distract them.

When someone is putting it is also important
to make sure that your *shadow* is not along the line
or path of their putt.

Term Time

AWAY: The player that is farthest from the hole.

DIVOT: A small piece of the ground taken up during a swing.

FORE!!: A word yelled when your ball is in danger of hitting another golfer.

HONOR: The privilege of hitting first from the tee. This is determined by the lowest score on the previous hole, or by a coin toss for the first hole.

PLAYING THROUGH: When a faster group of golfers passes a slower group of golfers with the golfers permission.

TENDING-THE-FLAG: When someone holds the flag in the hole so you can see where the hole is and immediately removes it when you hit the ball.

CHAPTER 6
GOLF SHOTS

When golfing you use different types of golf shots when hitting the ball toward the hole. Let's take a look at what these shots are.

PUTTING

The *putting shot* is used only when you are on or within a few feet of the putting green. The club to use when putting is the *putter*.

When putting you are not trying to hit the ball great distances; therefore, you do not need to make a big swing. The object is to roll the ball in or close to the hole. So for this stroke, your arms and the putter should move back and forth like a pendulum of a grandfather clock.

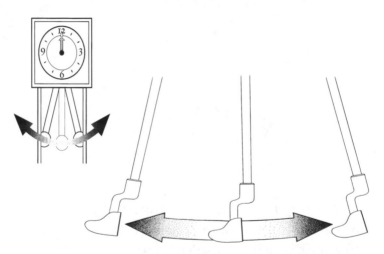

FUN FACT: Did you know the putting shot is the shot used most when golfing. For the average golfer four out of every ten shots in golf are putts. Therefore, if you can learn to be a good putter you can improve your golf game quicker.

The Putting Stroke

1

2

3

CHIP AND ROLL

The chip and roll shot is used when you are close to the green. The object of this shot is to land the ball on the green first, then have the ball roll to the hole.

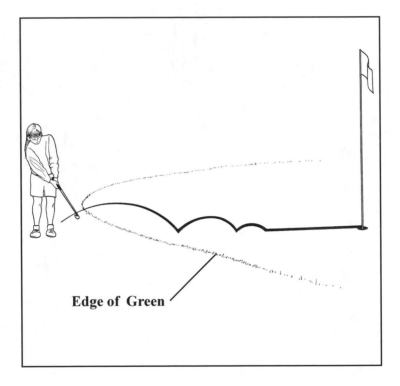

Edge of Green

When playing a chip and roll shot you will use different numbered irons around the green depending on how far you want to <u>carry</u> the ball to the green and how far you want to <u>roll</u> the ball on the green. The illustration below shows how you may use a different club from the same location to hit your ball onto the green.

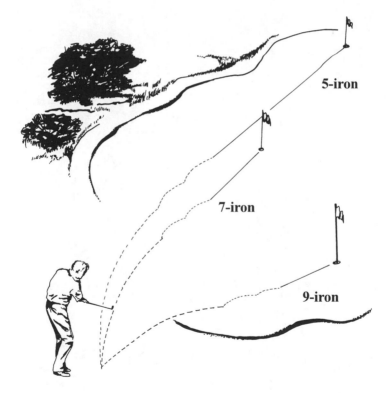

THE CHIP AND ROLL

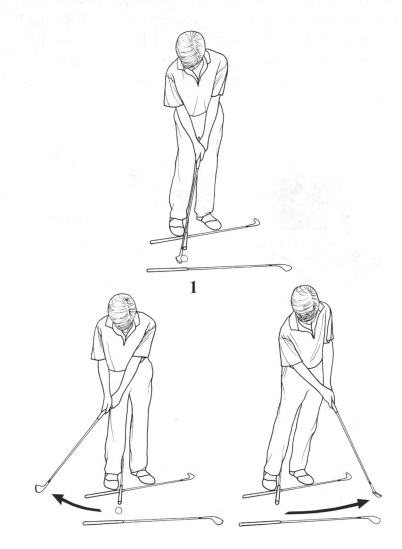

1

2   3

THE PITCH SHOT

The pitch shot is used when you want to hit the ball high in the air and have it roll very little after it lands on the green. For example, if you are close to the green and there is a bunker between you and the green, then you will need to pitch the ball over the bunker and onto the green. For this shot you should use a club that will help get the ball into the air easily. This would be a club with a high *loft*. Two good clubs for this type of shot are called the *Sand Wedge* and the *Pitching Wedge*.

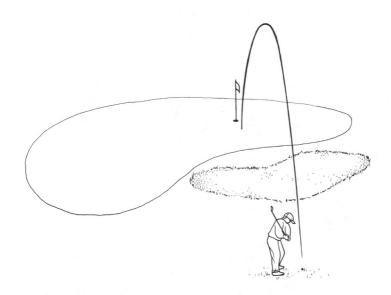

THE BUNKER SHOT

There are two types of bunker shots, *fairway* bunker shots and *greenside* bunker shots. Fairway bunker shots are made when your ball lands in a bunker along the fairway. Greenside bunker shots are made when your ball lands in a bunker next to the green. When starting, bunker shots are often harder to hit than other shots, so try to avoid any bunker.

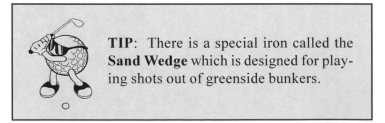

TIP: There is a special iron called the **Sand Wedge** which is designed for playing shots out of greenside bunkers.

THE FULL SWING (woods & irons)

    With full swing shots the ball will often curve in different directions. These shots are given specific names. For a right handed golfer a shot that curves left is called a *draw* or *hook*. A shot that curves right is called a *fade* or a *slice*. For a left handed golfer it is the opposite

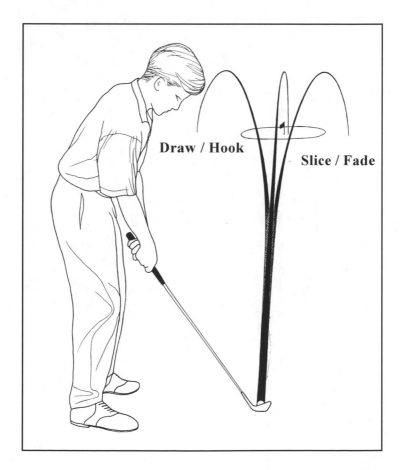

Draw / Hook   Slice / Fade

THE FULL SWING

When golfing you often need to advance the ball great distances toward your target. In order to do this you must make a *full swing.* You can hit full swing shots different heights and distances by using different woods or irons.

3

2

1

4

5

6

7

TERM TIME

APPROACH SHOT: The shot hit onto the green.

BACKSPIN: Spin put on the ball that helps it stop after it lands on the green.

CHIP SHOT: A short, low shot to the green.

DRAW: A shot that curves slightly from right to left, for a right handed golfer.

FADE: A shot that curves slightly from the left to the right, for a right handed golfer.

HOOK: A shot that curves from the right to the left, for a right handed golfer.

PULLED SHOT: A shot that travels straight, but straight left of the target, for a right handed golfer.

PUNCH SHOT: A low, short shot hit using less than a full-swing.

PUSHED SHOT: A shot that travels straight, but straight right of the target, for a right handed golfer.

CHAPTER 7
READY ... SET ... GO!
SHOT PREPARATION-
THE GRIP

To hit good golf shots you should start by learning how to properly *prepare* for each shot. Just like if you want to do well on a test in school you must properly prepare by doing your homework before the test.

In this chapter you will learn how to properly grip the golf club. In the next chapter you will learn the correct body posture, where to put the ball between your feet and how to aim your body when hitting the ball. These four fundamentals are called the *grip, posture, ball position,* and *alignment*. **Learning a proper grip is so important, we are going to take this entire chapter to learn the correct way to grip the golf club.**

GRIPPING THE GOLF CLUB

How you position your hands on the golf club is referred to as the *grip*. *Your grip on the golf club will affect the position of your clubface when you hit the golf ball. The position of the clubface then affects the direction the ball will travel.* Remember the sequence below:

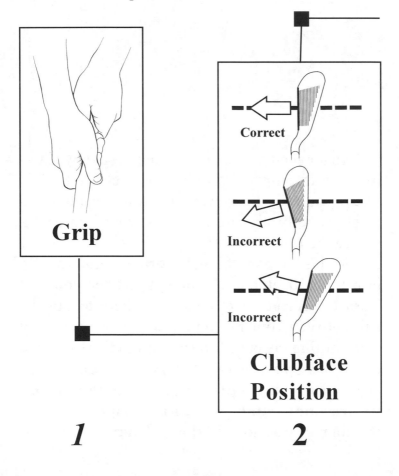

Grip

Correct

Incorrect

Incorrect

Clubface Position

1   *2*

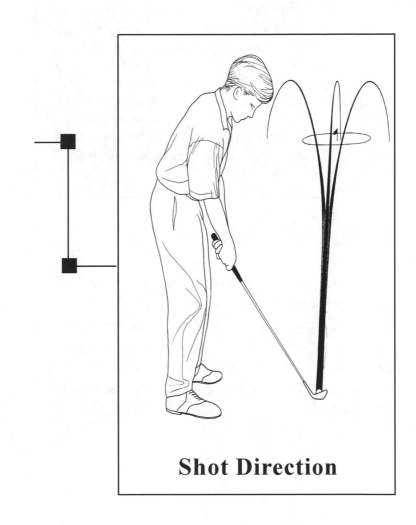

Shot Direction

3

GRIP TENSION

TIP: When gripping the golf club do not hold the club too tight. Imagine the grip of the the golf club as an egg. When holding an egg in your hand you would want to hold it tight enough so you do not drop it, but not so tight that you would break the shell of the egg. The same thing applies when gripping the golf club. Hold the club just tight enough to control it.

TYPES OF GRIPS

There are different ways to grip a golf club. The grip for putting is often different than the grip for full-swing shots. The illustration on the next page shows three of the most popular putting grips. Look closely at each grip. Try putting with each grip to determine which grip feels most comfortable for you.

PUTTING GRIPS

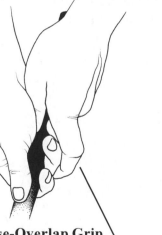

Ten-Finger Grip

With the Ten-Finger grip, all ten fingers are on the club, with your hands placed next to each other.

Reverse-Overlap Grip

This is the most popular grip. Notice the left index finger is off the club and placed down the outside of your fingers on your right hand.

Cross-Hand Grip

The Cross-Hand grip is the same as the Ten-Finger grip, but your hands are crossed. Your left hand is below your right hand. For a right handed golfer.

One important difference between the putting grip and the full swing grip is where you put your thumbs on the club. When gripping the club to putt, both of your thumbs should always go down the center of the grip. When gripping the club for the full swing shot, your thumbs go to the side of the center of the grip.

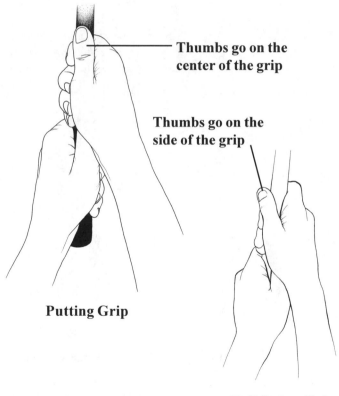

Thumbs go on the center of the grip

Thumbs go on the side of the grip

Putting Grip

Full Swing Grip

FULL SWING GRIPS

Like putting, there are different ways to grip the club for full swing shots as well. The illustration below shows the three different types of grips for the full swing. See if you can see the difference in each grip.

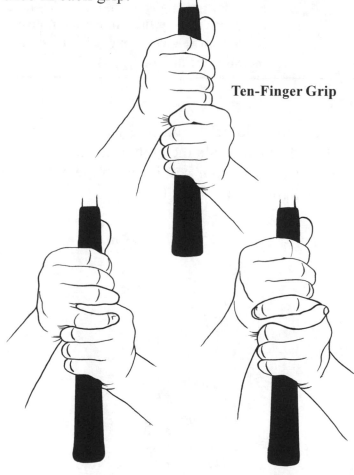

Ten-Finger Grip

Overlapping Grip   **Interlocking Grip**

GRIPPING THE GOLF CLUB

NOTE: Now it is time for you to follow along and actually practice each step as we discuss it. Remember, the directions will be given for golfing right-handed. If you are going to play the game of golf left-handed, when you read left or right in the text, do the opposite.

Start by holding the club in your left hand as illustrated below. Hold the club on an angle where your fingers meet your hand, **not** in the palm like you would hold a baseball bat.

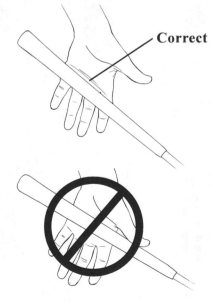

Correct

You will have better control and feel of the golf club by holding the club in your fingers. Think of writing with a pencil. It is much easier to control the pencil with your fingers than with your palm.

Next, make sure the soft padded area of your palm is on top of the grip. Practice gripping the club with the last three fingers of your left hand while keeping the soft padded area of your palm on top of the club.

The pad on your hand goes on the top of the grip.

When you put your thumb to the grip, make sure you put your thumb to the side of the center. Also, keep your thumb on the grip and not off the side of the grip when holding the club.

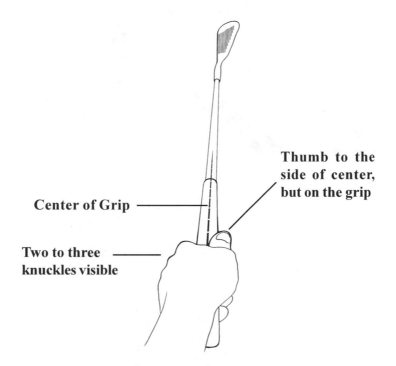

Thumb to the side of center, but on the grip

Center of Grip

Two to three knuckles visible

TIP: If you grip the club correctly you should see two or three knuckles on your left hand when holding the club as shown above. Can you count 2-3 knuckles on your left hand when you grip the club?

When adding your right hand to the grip, put the club in the fingers of your right hand as shown.

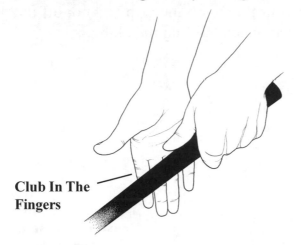

Club In The Fingers

Finally, cover your left thumb with the middle of your right palm.

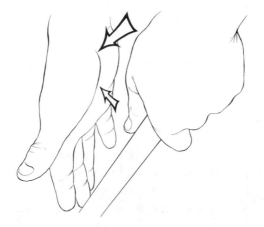

The lines formed by your thumbs should always point over your right shoulder as shown below.

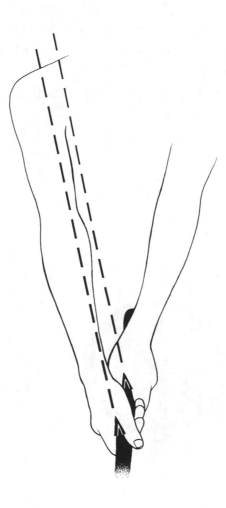

Many children grip the club by turning their right hand under the club as shown below in figure A. This exposes a majority of the left thumb. Children often grip the club as shown in figure A because they do not have the strength to control the club when holding it with their right hand covering the left thumb. For younger children this is fine. But, if you are 11 years or older, your right hand should start covering your left thumb as shown in figure B.

Figure B
A Proper Grip

Figure A

A simple key to remember is, as you get older you should see less of your left thumb and thumb nail. You should also see less of your right fingers and finger nails. Grip the golf club then look into a mirror and see if your grip looks like the grip illustrated below.

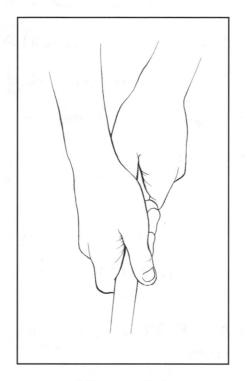

A Proper Grip

TERM TIME

ACE: Hitting the first shot from the tee into the hole, also referred to as a hole-in-one. (Very few golfers ever score a hole-in-one.)

BACK NINE OR BACK SIDE: The last nine holes of an eighteen hole course, also called the in-nine.

BIRDIE: A score of one under par on a hole.

BOGEY: A score of one over par on a hole.

DOUBLE BOGEY: A score of two over par.

DOUBLE EAGLE: A score of three under par. (Like the hole-in-one, few golfers ever score a double eagle as well).

EAGLE: A score of two under par on a hole.

FRONT NINE OR FRONT SIDE: The first nine holes in a round of golf.

MAKING THE TURN: The point during a round of golf when a group has just finished the first nine holes and is yet to start the second nine holes.

PAR: As score of excellence on a hole. There is a par for each hole, and a total par for the nine or eighteen holes. Par is determined by the length of the hole.

CHAPTER 8
SHOT PREPARATION
BODY POSTURE,
BALL POSITION AND
ALIGNMENT

BODY POSTURE

Your body posture in golf should be similar to other sports like baseball, basketball, and tennis. Your knees should be slightly bent and your back straight. As you bend toward the ground, bend at the waist keeping your back straight.

The Body Posture In Golf Is Similar To Other Sports

The following illustrations show three steps to good golfing posture. See if you can follow the three steps.

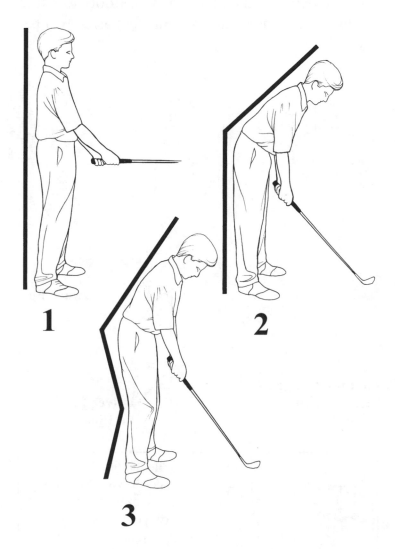

BALL POSITION

Where the ball is positioned between your feet is very important. The ball should always be in the area between the inside of your foot closest to the target and the center of your feet as shown below.

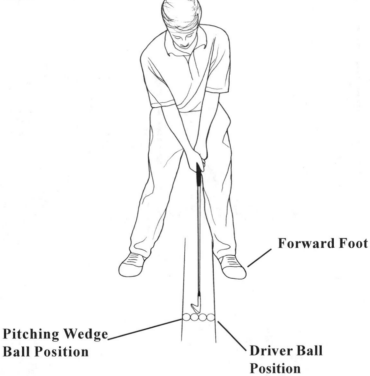

Forward Foot

Pitching Wedge Ball Position

Driver Ball Position

TIP: For proper ball position, start with the Driver off the inside of your foot closest to the target. Then, move the ball towards the center of your feet as your clubs get shorter in length.

ALIGNMENT

How you align your club and body to the golf ball and target is important. To start, imagine setting your club behind the golf ball on an imaginary line to the target called the *target line*.

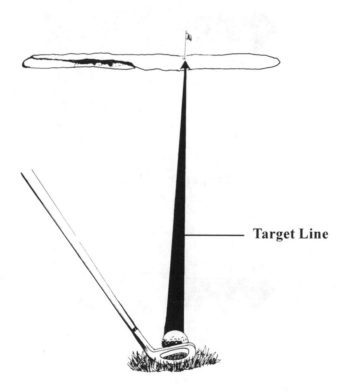

Target Line

Next, when standing to the side of the golf
ball, as you set your golf club behind the ball, the
bottom edge of the club and the target line should
form a <u>sideways letter T</u>.

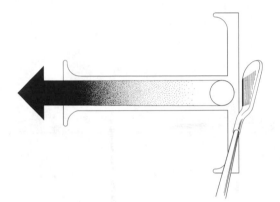

Proper Iron Alignment

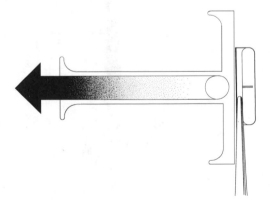

Proper Putter Alignment

Since you are standing to the side of the golf ball, you want to line your body to the side of your target. Therefore, align your body <u>parallel</u> to your target. **Do not align your body at the target, because this will align the club to the right of the target.**

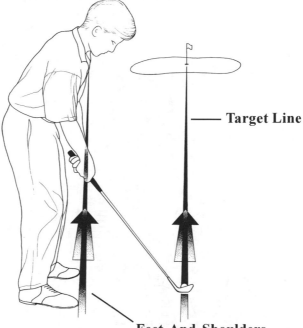

— Target Line

**Feet And Shoulders
Parallel To The Target**

FUN FACT: Did you know that nine out of every ten golfers aim their body incorrectly? Remember, your body should be aimed parallel to your target and the club should be aimed at your target.

An easy way to remember correct alignment is to imagine hitting a golf ball down a railroad track. When setting up, your club should be lined up with one rail, while your body is lined up with the other rail. This helps you to remember to line your body parallel with the target and not directly at the target.

Target Line

CHAPTER 9
THE FULL SWING
WOODS & IRONS

In this chapter you will learn the basics of the full swing. As mentioned earlier, a full swing is used when you need to hit the ball a long way. When making a full swing you will be using either a wood or an iron.

THE FULL SWING

BACK SWING

The first part of the full swing is called the *back swing*. The second part of the swing is called the *down swing* or *forward swing*.

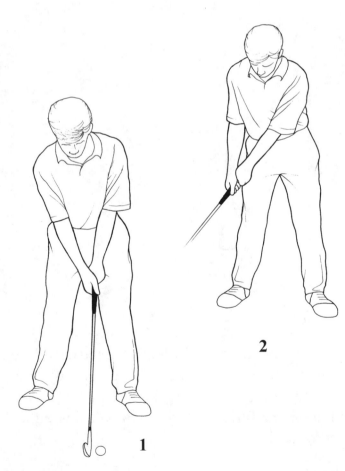

2

1

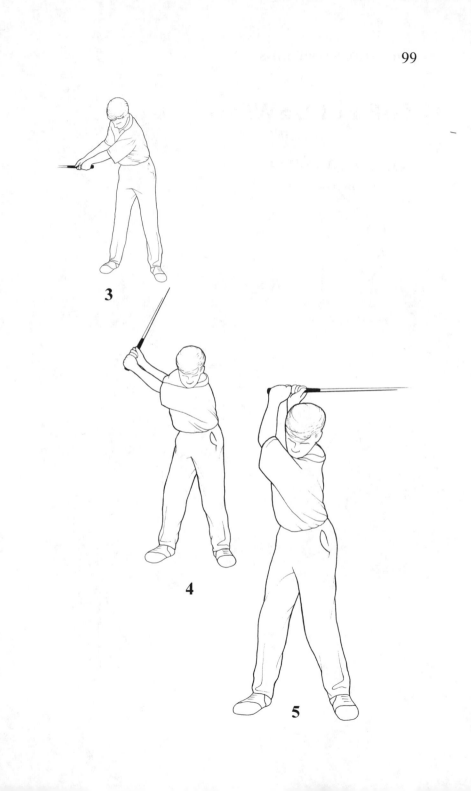

3

4

5

THE FULL SWING

FORWARD SWING

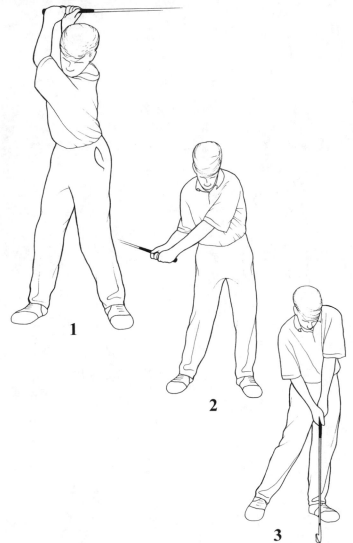

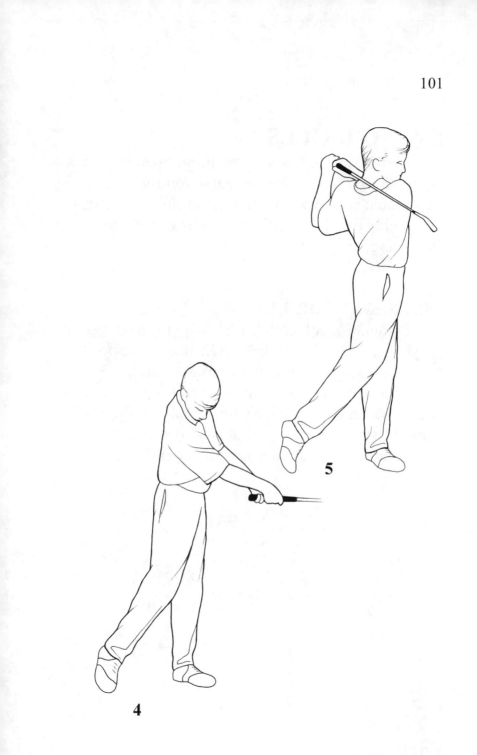

SWING DRILLS

Drills can help you learn the proper way to swing the golf club. They teach you the feeling you should have when swinging the club correctly. The following three drills will help you learn the full swing.

THE BUCKET DRILL

Swinging a golf club is like swinging a bucket. As shown below, hold a bucket in an upward position, pretending there is water in the bucket. For the backswing, rotate your body to the right and dump the water over your right shoulder. For the forward swing, rotate your body to the left and dump the water over your left shoulder.

 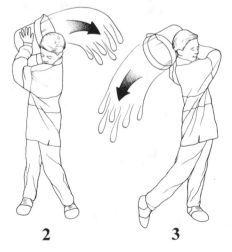

1   **2**   **3**

THUMBS UP DRILL

Another good drill is the *Thumbs-Up Drill*. As you turn, and your hands reach waist height, you should have your thumbs pointing to the sky for both the backswing and forward swing. This drill is pictured below. The saying to remember is "*thumbs to the sky at waist high*".

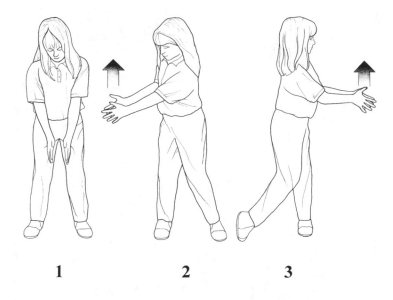

1   **2**   **3**

TIP: When swinging the golf club, imagine turning your back to the target on the back swing and turning your chest to the target on the forward swing.

TOE UP DRILL

After you have practiced the *Thumbs-Up* drill try it with the golf club. Just as your thumbs pointed up in the last drill, the *toe* of the club should point *up* at waist height.

1   2

When making a full swing imagine being on a weight scale. You start the swing by having your weight evenly distributed on both feet. As you swing back most of your weight moves to your back foot. As you swing forward most of your weight moves to your forward foot.

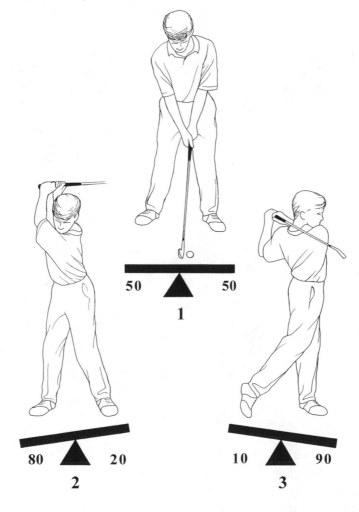

CHAPTER 10
TIPS "FORE" PLAYING AND PRACTICING

PLAYING TIPS

LEARN FROM A GOLFER
When you first start playing golf, play with an adult or a golfer that has experience so they can help you with basics of the game.

MAKE TEE RESERVATIONS
Always call the course before going to play, to make sure there are times available to play. It is suggested to make a *tee reservation* before going to the golf course.

PLAY WHEN THE COURSE IS NOT BUSY
If you are new to the game, try to play the golf course at off-peak times. You can call the course beforehand to see what times are best for junior golfers to play.

DO NOT WORRY ABOUT YOUR SCORE

As a young golfer, do not worry about your golf scores. Golf is a game that can be difficult to learn. It is more important to become familiar with the game of golf and enjoy playing the game. If you enjoy golf you will get better as you play more.

PLAY FROM THE CORRECT SET OF TEES

When starting each hole, tee off from a location that suites your abilities. The following guidelines suggest where you should tee the ball.

Age	Tee Location
7 & under	Never more than 100 yards from the green.
8 & 9	At the beginning of the fairway
10-11	The forward most tees
12 & above	The set of tees that suites your ability, provided you do not slow up play

** You may have to vary this based on individual abilities.

LIMIT YOUR STROKES

Limit your strokes when playing the game. When starting, it is okay to limit your strokes to nine or ten per hole. If you are not on the green after six or seven shots, then you should place the ball on the green. Also, limit yourself to four putts per hole when starting.

IMPROVE YOUR LIE WHEN STARTING

When first learning the game, improve the lie of the ball on the ground so you have a chance to hit a good shot. As your skills improve you will learn how to hit the ball from where the ball lies without moving it.

LET FASTER GROUPS PLAY THROUGH

If the group in front of you is playing faster than you, you should let them *play through.* When letting a group play through, move to a safe location so you do not get hit by the ball.

SPEED OF PLAY

Your speed of play is very important when golfing. You should always play 9-holes in two hours or less, or average approximately 13 minutes per hole. You do not want to have to run around the golf course, but you should play knowing there is not unlimited time. The following tips will help you play in the proper amount of time.

KEEP PACE

When on the golf course, if your group keeps up with the group in front of you, or if you play each hole in 13 minutes or less, you will normally not have to worry about slowing up the groups behind you.

DON'T WASTE TIME

Limit your practice swings to one per shot.

Walk quickly between golf shots.

Go directly to the next tee after completing each hole.

Watch your shot and your playing partners shots till they land, and mark the location where the ball lands in your mind.

Never record your score on or near the green of the hole last played, but rather on the next tee.

When approaching the green place your golf bag on the side of the green closest to the next tee.

Do not spend too much time looking for your golf ball if it is hard to find.

SCORING

Like other sports, you may keep score when playing golf. The lower the score the better. There are different names for different scores, with each based on a comparison to par. *Remember, par is a "score of excellence" on a hole.*

Eagle
A score of two-under par for a hole. Eagles are rare for any golfer.

Birdie
A score of one-under par for a hole. Birdies are rare when beginning.

Par
A score of par for a hole.

Bogey
A score of one-over par for a hole.

Double Bogey
A score of two-over par for a hole.

Triple Bogey
A score of three-over par for a hole.

Quadruple Bogey
A score of four-over par for a hole.

THE SCORECARD

The scorecard provides a place to keep your score, states the length and par of every hole, and often shows an illustration of each hole. The illustration shows the make up of each hole to give you information on how to play the hole. You should always pick-up a scorecard and pencil in the golf shop before playing.

Hole
Layout ——

Length —— Of Hole	Blue 69.9/116	360	385	405	405	332	150	196	389	525	3147
	White 69.9/116	348	370	401	392	320	140	180	383	496	3030
	Handicap	11	1	3	7	9	17	13	5	15	
Par ————	Par	4	4	4	4	4	3	3	4	5	35
Players —— Names And Scores											
	Hole	1	2	3	4	5	6	7	8	9	OUT
	Par	4	4	5	4	4	3	3	4	5	36
	Red 70.0/118	344	225	401	375	306	133	166	322	447	2719
	Handicap	7	13	15	1	5	17	9	3	11	

Date:_____Scorer:_____

The scorecard below shows the number of strokes Mike had for each hole. Can you determine whether Mike hand an eagle, birdie, par, bogey, double bogey, triple bogey or quadruple bogey on each hole?

HOLE	10	11	12	13	14	15	16	17	18	IN	TOTAL
PAR	4	4	3	5	4	3	4	4	5	36	
Mike	4	8	4	3	4	2	6	7	4	42	

DATE: 6/3   SCORER: *Amy Smith*   ATTEST: *Mike Jones*

Answers:
10) Par 11) Quadruple Bogey 12) Bogey 13) Eagle 14) Par 15) Birdie 16) Double Bogey 17) Triple Bogey 18) Birdie

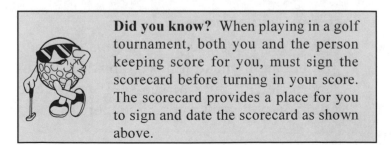

Did you know? When playing in a golf tournament, both you and the person keeping score for you, must sign the scorecard before turning in your score. The scorecard provides a place for you to sign and date the scorecard as shown above.

PRACTICE TIPS

SAFETY FIRST

When practicing, always make sure you are hitting away from people or any objects that could get damaged if the ball hits it. Also, always makes sure there is no one behind you before swinging the club.

AIM AT A TARGET

When playing the game of golf you must hit the ball towards a specific target. Therefore, when practicing, alway practice hitting to a specific target. Get in the habit of hitting to different targets every five shots.

PRACTICE ALL AREAS OF THE GAME

Most golfers spend all their time practicing just the full swing with their woods and irons. Did you know six out of every ten shots in golf are from within 60 yards of the green. Therefore, make sure you practice all the different shots in the game.

MAKE PRACTICE FUN

Be creative and use your imagination when practicing to make it more fun while learning different types of shots. If practice is fun you will want to practice more.

PLACE YOUR EQUIPMENT PROPERLY

To reduce the chance of injury or damage to your equipment, place your equipment in the correct location when playing or practicing. Never put your equipment or practice balls directly to your side as shown below.

Incorrect

Correct

TERM TIME

GREENS FEE: The term representing the cost to play a round of golf.

LIE: The position of the ball on the ground.

MATCH PLAY: A competition between teams or individuals by hole, where the winner has the lowest score on the most holes.

MEDAL OR STROKE PLAY: A competition where the individual with the fewest strokes or lowest total score is the winner.

MULLIGAN: When a player hits a second ball off the first tee because they did not like their first shot. Although many golfers do this, it is not allowed during a golf tournament.

PIN HIGH: When your ball lands at the same distance as the pin, but to the side of the pin.

CHAPTER 11
COMMON QUESTIONS
FROM KIDS AND
PARENTS

Like any other activity, parents and their children often have many questions regarding the do's and don'ts about learning the game of golf. This chapter will help answer some of the most common questions you may have.

When should a child start to play the game of golf?

A child is ready to start learning about the game of golf when they are old enough to walk around with a club in their hand. Naturally when they are under five they will do more watching and following. As they get older and stronger they can play and practice more. When starting the game, a child may begin by just putting on the putting green from close to the hole, then gradually work back from the hole and hit more shots.

When should your son or daughter get started taking golf lessons?

Learning the game of golf is a lifelong process. The sooner you can start children in any golf instructional program, the better. The key is to make sure the instruction content matches the age and ability of the child. Simple instruction can start as early as six or seven years of age, to start getting children comfortable with being on the golf course.

Golf seems like a serious game. Should we make sure our children follow this thought?

There are rules and proper etiquette to follow when playing golf. However, the game of golf should also be fun and recreational. Do not put to much pressure on children to always try harder and be serious on the golf course. Let them just enjoy hitting the golf ball, being outdoors, interacting with friends and family and learning a game that requires some disipline. If a child is competitive and wants to improve their skills they will normally express it.

Where can we get golf instruction for children.
Check with a local golf facility to see which facilities have a golf professional that is a member of the (PGA) Professional Golfers Association of America. Most PGA golf professionals are trained and qualified to teach. In addition, check with friends and other sources to find out which professionals are best qualified. There is a wide range in qualifications even among PGA Golf Professionals teaching. Getting a good, qualified golf instructor can make a big difference in the development of a young golfer.

How often should children get golf instruction?
To maximize ones potential, a golfer should get continuous instruction. At a competitive level a young golfer should be getting instruction weekly or bi-weekly, so the professional can continue to monitor progress, and work on different areas of the game. Do not have your children working with numerous instructors. Select an instructor that can work with your child on a regular basis and develop a good relationship.

What should our child do in the off season?

Make sure you give your children a chance to play other sports and do other activities in the off-season. It is important to give children a chance to experience more than just golf.

The off-season is also a good time to make swing changes for many golfers. As children get to the middle school age, the off-season is a great time to start working on improving swing fundamentals without worrying about the flight of the ball. This gives the child time to get comfortable with the different feeling that accompanies changes.

As a teenager you can start a supervised weight training program to improve your strength and conditioning in the off-season.

When should children start to compete in golf tournaments?

Children can start competing in golf tournaments at a young age. Some tournaments have age brackets for children as young as five. Tournaments should be looked at as a way to help introduce and teach children how to play the game. However, do not have your children enter a golf tournment until they have been on the golf course a couple dozen times, so they are familiar with the game. Remember it can be difficult for children under eight or nine years of age to even hit the golf ball. Do not enter your child into a golf tournament until they are physically strong enough to swing the club and they are comfortable playing the game of golf.

How do you find out about local youth golf programs or golf tournaments?
Contact your local golf professional, golf facility or your local newspapers. Communities often have local golf associations with instruction and tournament opportunties.

PGA SECTIONAL OFFICES
The Sectional Offices for the Professional Golfers Association of America are listed below. You may contact your local office to get additional information about junior golf programs in your area.

Aloha: Honolulu, Hawaii; 808-593-2230
Carolinas: N. Myrtle Beach, S.C.; 803-399-2742
Central New York: Syracuse, NY; 315-468-6812
Colorado: Aurora, Colorado; 303-745-3697
Connecticut: Rocky Hill, Connecticut; 860-257-4653
Dixie: Birmingham, Alabama; 205-822-0321
Gateway: St Louis, Missouri; 314-991-4994
Georgia: Marietta, Georgia; 770-952-9063
Gulf States: New Orleans, Louisiana; 800-469-9199
Illinois: Lemont, Illinois; 630-257-9671
Indiana: Franklin, Indiana; 317-738-9696
Iowa: Cedar Rapids, Iowa; 319-378-9142
Kentucky: Louisville, Kentucky; 502-499-7422
Metro New York: New Rochele, NY; 914-347-2325

Michigan: Livonia, Michigan; 3-1-522-2323
Middle Atlantic: Columbia, Maryland; 703-551-4653
Midwest: Blue Springs, Missouri; 816-229-6565
Minnesota: Coon Rapids, Minnesota; 612-754-8020
Nebraska: Lincoln, Nebraska; 402-489-7760
New England: Wakefield, Massachusitts; 508-664-6555
New Jersey: Jamesburg, New Jersey; 908-521-4000
North Florida: Daytona Beach, Florida; 904-322-0899
Northeastern New York: Albany, NY 518-463-3067
Northern California: Livermore, CA; 510-455-7800
Northern Ohio: Willoughby, Ohio; 216-951-4546
Northern Texas: Plano, Texas; 972-881-4653
Pacific Northwest: Olympia, Washington; 800-688-4653
Philadelphia: Norristown, PA; 610-277-5777
Rockey Mountain: Eagle, Idaho; 208-939-6028
South Central: Broken Arrow, Oklahoma; 918-357-3328
South Florida: Coral Spring, Florida; 954-752-9299
Southern California: Brea, California 714-776-4653
Southern Ohio: Columbus, Ohio; 614-221-7194
Southern Texas: The Woodlands, Texas; 281-363-0511
Southwest: Scottsdale, Arizona; 602-443-9002
Sun Country: Albuquerque, NM; 505-271-1442
Tennessee: Franklin, Tennessee; 615-790-7600
Tri-State: Monaca, Pennsylvannia; 412-774-2224
Utah: Salt Lake City, Utah; 801-281-8123
Western New York: Williamsville, NY; 716-626-0603
Wisconsin: Milwaukee, Wisconsin; 414-365-4479

Well kids!! I hope you enjoyed your golf lesson with Coach Ruthenberg and I!! It was a lot of fun giving you some tips to help your golf game.

Don't forget to enter the contest to give me a name. Simply complete the entry form below and return it to: RGS Publishing; P.O. Box 25021; Lansing, Michigan 48909. Or fax your entry to 517-347-2665. I look forward to seeing you at the golf course.

<u>NAME OUR FRIEND CONTEST</u>

NAME: _____

ADDRESS: _____

CITY: _____

STATE: _____   **ZIP:** _____

PHONE: _____

NAME (CHOICE #1) _____

NAME (CHOICE #2) _____

Closing Thoughts
by Coach Ruthenberg

It has been fun teaching you about the great game of golf. Since I was a young boy I have been truly fascinated by this game. The golf course has always been a special place for me. As a kid I enjoyed playing Maple Lanes Golf Courses in Sterling Heights, Michigan with my brothers and great golfing buddies John Schlaman and Bob Downs. Something about the beauty of the course in the early morning or evening, the joy of a great golf shot and the company of great people, makes golf truly special.

I recommend you contact your local PGA Golf Professional to help you learn the game. Also, I invite you to visit our golf ball friend and I, at one of America's finest teaching centers - *The Golf Center at Michigan State University*. Each summer we provide an exciting lineup of golf camps headed by Michigan State University Men's Golf Coach Ken Horvath. You may receive additional information about the golf camps and other instructional programs at *The Golf Center at Michigan State University* by calling 517-355-1635.

In closing, I hope *Golf Fore Kids* leads you to many special golf moments.